MUSIC MINUS ONE TUBA

PACIFIC COAST HORNS

VOLUME 3

Brass Quintets for Tuba

4709

SUGGESTIONS FOR USING THIS MMO EDITION

WE HAVE TRIED to create a product that will provide you an easy way to learn and perform these compositions with a full ensemble in the comfort of your own home. The following MMO features and techniques will help you maximize the effectiveness of the MMO practice and performance system:

Because it involves a fixed accompaniment performance, there is an inherent lack of flexibility in tempo. We have observed generally accepted tempi, and always in the originally intended key, but some may wish to perform at a different tempo, or to slow down or speed up the accompaniment for practice purposes; or to alter the piece to a more comfortable key. For maximum flexibility, you can purchase from MMO specialized CD players & recorders which allow variable speed while maintaining proper pitch, and vice versa. This is an indispensable tool for the serious musician and you may wish to look into purchasing this useful piece of equipment for full enjoyment of all your MMO editions.

We want to provide you with the most useful practice and performance accompaniments possible. If you have any suggestions for improving the MMO system, please feel free to contact us. You can reach us by e-mail at *info@musicminusone.com*.

4709

CONTENTS

Tuba

Alexander's Ragtime Band

By IRVING BERLIN
Arrangement by PAUL CHAUVIN

MMO 4709

43

48

Solo

53

61

66

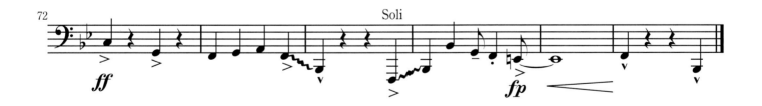

72

Soli

Tuba

The Toy Trumpet

Music by RAYMOND SCOTT
Arrangement by CHARLES WARREN

Tuba

Stompin' at the Savoy

Tuba

The Original, First and Foremost Version of:

The Blue Danube

the mistake waltz
by JOHANN STRAUSS, JR.
Arrangement by PAUL CHAUVIN

Tuba

Mysterious Mose

Words and Music by
WALTER DOYLE and TED WEEMS

Tuba

Harlem Nocturne

Words by DICK ROGERS
Music by EARLE HAGEN
Arrangement by PAUL CHAUVIN

Bugle Call Rag

Tuba

by JACK PETTIS, BILLY MYERS
and ELMER SCHOEBEL
Arrangement by CHARLES WARREN

Tuba

Les Toreadors
from CARMEN

By GEORGE BIZET
Arrangement by CHARLES WARREN

Tuba

Caravan
from SOPHISTICATED LADIES

Blue Rondo A La Turk

Tuba

By DAVE BRUBECK
Arrangement by CHARLES WARREN

Tuba

Amazing Grace

Tuba

William Tell Overture

MUSIC MINUS ONE
50 Executive Boulevard
Elmsford, New York 10523-1325
1.800.669.7464 (U.S.)/914.592.1188 (International)

www.musicminusone.com
e-mail: info@musicminusone.com